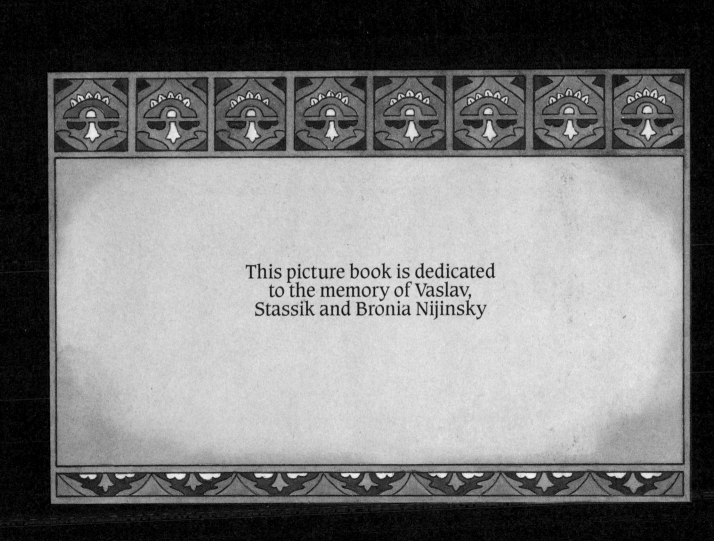

This picture book is dedicated
to the memory of Vaslav,
Stassik and Bronia Nijinsky

The author wishes to thank for their help and advice:
Marina Vivien, Curator of the Museum,
Vaganova School of Choreography, Leningrad, USSR;
Maureen Perrie; Janet Richards; Derek Parfit; Penny Jowitt;
David Elliott and the Southern Arts Association for their travel bursary to the USSR

Special thanks to Andrew Brighton for his involvement.

Published by Doubleday, a division of
Bantam Doubleday Dell Publishing Group, Inc.
666 Fifth Avenue, New York, New York 10103

Doubleday and the portrayal of an anchor
with a dolphin are trademarks of
Doubleday, a division of Bantam Doubleday Dell Publishing Group, Inc.

Library of Congress Cataloging-in-Publication Data
Brighton, Catherine.
Nijinsky: scenes from the childhood of a great dancer/
Catherine Brighton.—1st ed. in the U.S.A.
p.   cm.
Summary: Describes how the renowned Russian ballet dancer found an
outlet for his childhood unhappiness through dance and was
eventually called to perform for the Tsar.
ISBN 0-385-24663-3. ISBN 0-385-24926-8 (lib. bdg.)
1. Nijinsky, Waslaw, 1890–1950—Juvenile literature. 2. Ballet
dancers—Russian S.F.S.R.—Biography—Juvenile literature.
[1. Nijinsky, Waslaw, 1890–1950—Childhood and youth. 2. Ballet
dancers.] I. Title.
GV1785.N6B7 1989
792.8′2′0924—dc19
[B]
[92]   88-25721
CIP
AC

NIJINSKY

SCENES FROM THE CHILDHOOD OF THE GREAT DANCER

CATHERINE BRIGHTON

DOUBLEDAY
NEW YORK LONDON TORONTO SYDNEY AUCKLAND

TRAVELING

Not long ago in Russia, there lived three children, Stassik, Vaslav, and Bronia. Their parents, Thomas and Eleonora Nijinsky, were traveling dancers, so the children had no proper home.

Sometimes at night, they would go to sleep in a theater dressing room and wake next morning in a carriage on the road.

On their travels, the Nijinskys went from town to town all across Russia. They saw pine-covered mountains and glassy lakes. They saw barren plains and snow-covered wastes, and in the south they saw grapes on the vine and brilliant butterflies, which Vaslav chased with a huge net.

ON THE STAGE

Thomas taught his children to dance when they were very little. He taught them a Russian dance, and at Christmas, Stassik, Vaslav, and Bronia appeared for the very first time on a real stage.

Vaslav could jump high. The audience loved it and threw presents onto the stage. Flowers, sweets, and little toys rained down as the children took their bows. Afterward, in the dressing room, Eleonora shared out the presents to stop the children squabbling. Vaslav got a jack-in-the-box, which he played with for hours; she gave a clockwork mouse to Stassik, and Bronia had a Dutch doll.

WHITE NIGHTS IN NARVA

The Russian summer nights are very short.

On these white nights, the children wouldn't go to bed. Just like the sun, they refused to go down. So Thomas and Eleonora took them to the theater garden. There was a long veranda where people sat laughing and drinking. There were music and dancing, and Chinese lanterns were looped in the trees.

The children sat at a wooden table and ate piroshki. When they were sure no one was looking, they moved among the tables drinking the leftover wine from patterned glasses. They drunkenly chased one another, and Thomas and Eleonora found them, hours later, fast asleep on the lawn.

ALONE

But the children's life was not always happy.

One night, they heard Thomas and Eleonora arguing in the next room. Their voices were loud and angry. The children huddled together behind the door. They did not dare open it or call out because Thomas was banging the table as he shouted. At last the door to the apartment banged shut, and the night was still.

Vaslav's teeth were chattering, and he felt icy cold.

The children crept into the lighted room and went to their mother.

Thomas had left them, and now they were on their own.

ST. PETERSBURG

Now that Thomas had gone, Eleonora's dancing days were over. She and the children moved to a bleak apartment that overlooked a canal in the great city of St. Petersburg.

In the winter, the river and canals froze. Sometimes the snow was so thick that the old porter had to dig a path to open their door.

Vaslav, Stassik, and Bronia became expert firewood hunters. They pulled their sledge through the deserted streets collecting anything that Eleonora could burn in the stove.

DANCE LESSONS

In the evening, the fire crackled, and to keep them warm Eleonora gave the children dancing lessons. She could see that Vaslav danced as well as his father. Bronia, too, was dancing well. Eleonora saved enough money to buy Stassik an accordion, and he sat in the corner and played for them.

It was her greatest dream that one of her children should go to the Imperial Ballet School. If Vaslav could win a place, some of her money worries would be over.

# THE WALK TO THEATER STREET

One summer morning, Eleonora left Stassik and Bronia waiting at the window as she led Vaslav through the streets of St. Petersburg.

Today he must do his audition at the Imperial Ballet School.

He had been practicing his bow so that he would look smart in front of the examiners. He kept stopping to gaze at his reflection in the shop windows. People smiled as they passed.

VASLAV'S AUDITION

At the school, Eleonora waited anxiously as Vaslav was led through a door into the examination room.

A doctor examined his feet. He was weighed and measured, and more doctors listened to his heart and peered into his ears and down his throat.

"Do this. Do that. Walk this way. Walk that way. Arms up. Arms down."

"First position," said a man with a curly mustache.

At the end of the day, when he came back through the door to his mother, he had passed all the tests. He was now a pupil of the Imperial Ballet School.

Out in the street, Eleonora bought Vaslav a big green ice cream and a toy windmill each for Stassik and Bronia.

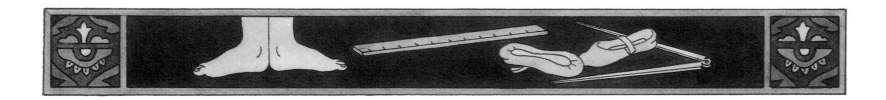

THE PREPARATION

Crackly leaves were falling in the streets and parks, and a cold wind was swirling up the Neva River.

At home, the chairs were covered by Vaslav's school uniform. He had more clothes now than he had ever had before. Bronia looked longingly at the six shirts, six undershirts, six pairs of pants, and the six pairs of socks with no sign of a hole. He had a gray coat for summer and one for winter with a fur collar. His uniform had the imperial insignia of a silver lyre embroidered on the collar. His hat had an eagle badge on it. In a box on the floor were his dancing clothes and soft leather ballet shoes.

Tomorrow was Vaslav's first day at the ballet school, and Eleonora sent the children to bed early.

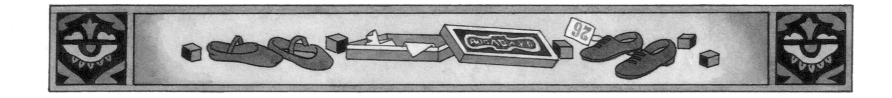

SCHOOL DAYS

Vaslav loved the dancing.

His teachers watched in awe as the tiny boy leapt through the air. But the other boys were jealous. They called him "Chinaman" because his dark eyes slanted. They called him "Polack" because his parents were Polish.

"But I'm Russian," Vaslav protested and fought back his tears.

One day, the other boys piled up chairs and benches to see how high Vaslav could leap. Higher and higher they moved the jump, until Vaslav toppled and fell. The terrified boys ran away. Hours later, a teacher found Vaslav bleeding and unconscious on the floor.

Suddenly the Imperial Ballet School was in an uproar. The teachers feared that their best pupil was going to die, and he was rushed to the hospital.

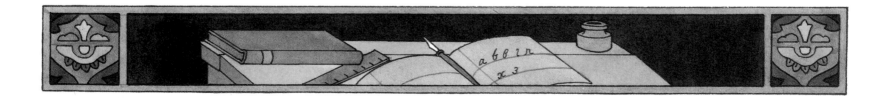

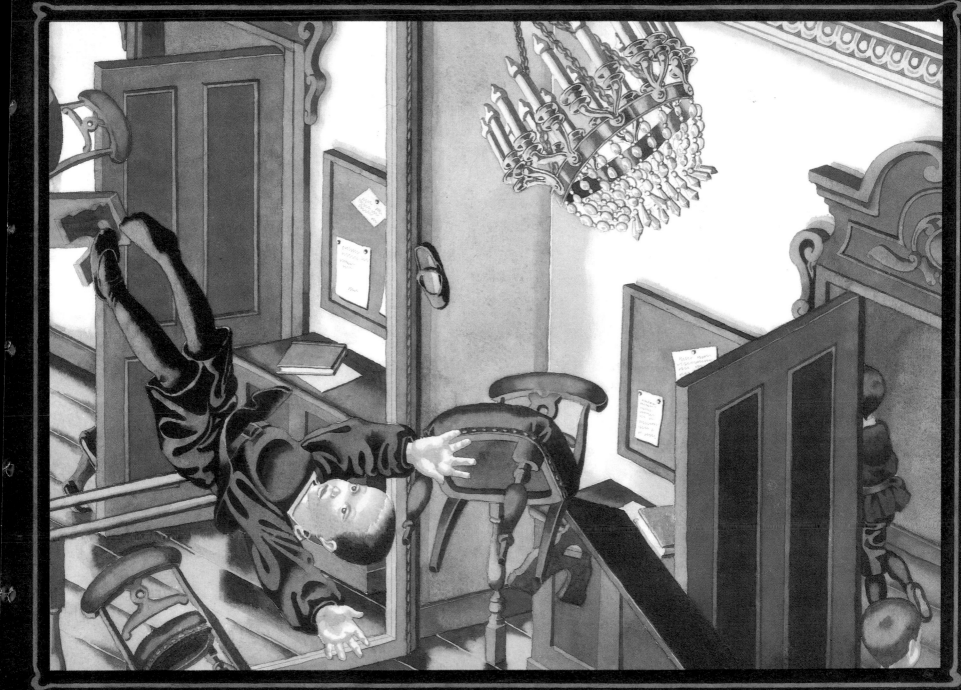

THE COURT HOSPITAL

Eleonora, Stassik, and Bronia stayed by Vaslav's bed for three days and three nights. The sun streamed across his bed, but still he did not move.

Eleonora was dozing in the chair when Bronia jumped up.

"Mamoussia! His eyes are open!"

Vaslav was awake and asking for water. The doctors hurried in. They didn't believe it. How could he possibly live with those injuries?

After two weeks, the boys from school were allowed to visit him. They were scared in case Vaslav had told on them.

They stood at the end of the bed nervously clutching flowers and fruit.

"You put soap on the floor," said Vaslav. "You wanted me to slip."

But he forgave them. After three months, Vaslav returned to the ballet school, and he had many new friends.

DANCING FOR THE CZAR

Soon Vaslav could leap as high as before. His teacher, Sergei Legat, gave him extra lessons so that Vaslav could dance a solo before the Czar himself in the end-of-school-year ballet.

Vaslav worked and practiced. Even at night before bed, he would hold his bed rail and gently stretch his legs.

After weeks of preparation, the big night arrived. Eleonora, Stassik, and Bronia arrived at the school in their best clothes. The children kept turning and wriggling to look up at Czar Nicholas. He sat with the Czarina, and they looked like the king and queen in fairy tales.

As Vaslav danced, the audience gasped. It seemed as if he stayed in the air for minutes before his magic feet touched the floor.

Bronia snuggled up to her mother, and at that moment they both knew that one day Vaslav would be a great dancer.

Many people believe that Vaslav Nijinsky was the greatest male ballet dancer that has ever lived.

He was famous throughout the world, for his dancing in ballets such as *Le Spectre de la Rose, Petrushka*, and *The Rite of Spring*.

Sadly, he danced for only ten years. Like his brother, Stassik, he became insane when he was a young man and could no longer dance.

Bronia Nijinskaya, Vaslav's sister, also attended the Imperial Ballet School. She, too, became a great dancer and choreographer. She gave us the ballets *Les Biches* and *Les Noces*. Bronia continued to be an important teacher until the end of her life.

921
Nij   Brighton, Catherine
            Nijinsky.

L